BEACON SERMON OUTLINE SERIES

# SERMON OUTLINES
## ON
# Advent &
# Christmas

## GENE WILLIAMS

Beacon Hill Press of Kansas City
Kansas City, Missouri

Copyright 2002
by Beacon Hill Press of Kansas City

ISBN 083-411-9862

Printed in the
United States of America

Cover Design: Paul Franitza

### Library of Congress Cataloging-in-Publication Data

Williams, Gene, 1932-
    Sermon outlines on Advent and Christmas / Gene Williams.
       p. cm. — (Beacon sermon outline series)
      ISBN 0-8341-1986-2
  1. Advent sermons—Outlines, syllabi, etc.  2. Christmas sermons—Outlines, syllabi, etc.
3. Bible—Sermons—Outlines, syllabi, etc. I. Title. II. Series.
    BV4254.5 W55 2002
    251'.61—dc21

                                 2002007691

10  9  8  7  6  5  4  3  2  1

# Contents

# INTRODUCTION

## Christmas Dinners for the Soul

When I was growing up, Christmas dinner at our house was always a special time. My mother would start preparing many weeks in advance. She would make all kinds of cakes and goodies. Then the week of Christmas she would gather in everything needed for a special meal. Even though we were anything but a wealthy family, we were going to do Christmas, and that meant a great dinner. There may not have been much under the tree, but there would be a feast on the table. No one would leave that table hungry. Mom lovingly and with much effort made sure we celebrated the coming of the Bread of Life. I believe that those who have the opportunity to feed the family of God should take advantage of that privilege and make Christmas a spiritual feasting time. At least put the food on the table. These outlines were prepared with that thought in mind.

Christmas is a wonderful time to lift up the message of Jesus, who is the Bread of Life. The excitement of the season can and should be transferred to His advent. It is highly possible to focus the minds of a Christmas-conscious people on the greatest Gift of all.

Across the years I have found it to be a wonderful experience to preach a series of messages beginning the Sunday after Thanksgiving that continue through the Sunday following Christmas. Instead of getting lost in the secularization of Christmas, take charge and make this a spiritual season. You will find that by focusing on Jesus for four or five Sundays, your people will become more Christ-centered.

This was the attitude with which each of these messages was first presented. These outlines are intended to be seeds that our Lord will bring to life in your fertile mind. Take them in the spirit with which they are given. You will need to do some expanding and most of all personalizing.

This pastor-preacher learned that the best preaching is wise in its simplicity. And I learned that people identify with our humanity. Use your own illustrations as often as possible.

You will notice that some passages of Scripture appear more than once in the different series. This is by design, since there is only one real Christmas story. We have approached the presentation of Christmas messages from several different perspectives in order to get all that God is saying through His Word.

One final bit of help—while most of these messages were presented in series form, they can be pulled out, adapted, and used in single form.

Feel free to substitute the suggested carols with those that may be more familiar to your congregation. The ones indicated are merely options for you to consider.

Take these seeds and plant them. Then water with prayer and see what God causes to grow!

# Part I

# MESSAGES ON THE SONGS OF CHRISTMAS

The purpose of this series is to look into the songs of Christmas and to lift out the special messages that will enhance the spiritual growth of our people when applied to their lives. You will find simple truths that can be adapted to any person's life. Thereby, Christmas becomes a season of receiving and enjoying God's greatest Gift.

# Mary's Song of Joy

## Luke 1:46-55

### Introduction

A. Christmas is a season of celebration, and music plays a key role in any experience of that kind. The music of Christmas is especially meaningful. Just listening to the words of the carols will give you a lift.

B. This Christmas season we will look at some of the biblical songs. There are four occasions when a song of praise is given priority in the scriptural accounts that relate to the coming of Jesus.
1. Mary's song—1:46-55
2. Zechariah's song—verses 67-79
3. The angels' song—2:8-20
4. Simeon's song—verses 21-35

C. On this first Sunday of Advent we will consider Mary's song of joy.
1. It is similar to the Old Testament psalms in that it is a hymn of praise for God's kindness.
2. It may very well be called a song of pure joy, for Mary has found reason to lift her voice in praise to God.
3. Read the scripture, 1:46-55.

D. We can learn much from Mary, who found great reason to praise God in spite of adverse circumstances.
1. There were many unanswered questions, verses 29-35.
2. Her position in the society of that day was very uncomfortable.
3. Mary still revealed a heart full of praise.

### I. Mary Is Joyful Because God's Promises Are Being Fulfilled Through Her

A. The promises of the past are fulfilled in God's pronouncement to her in verse 35.
1. The Jewish people had anticipated the coming Messiah.

2. God is now telling Mary that all of the promises will be fulfilled in the Child she is to deliver.
  B. Mary's song encourages us to have a positive attitude in life.
    1. Mary rejoiced because God was keeping His promise.
    2. We rejoice when we accept the fact that God still keeps His word.
  C. Mary's song of joy is the result of her realization that God's promise demonstrated that He had not forgotten Israel.

## II. Mary Is Filled with Praise Because of Four Divine Qualities That She Senses in God

  A. His holiness is revealed in verse 49.
    1. Holiness communicates ideas of sincerity, purity, and singleness of purpose.
    2. God is, therefore, faithful to His purposes and His promises.
  B. His mercy is found in verse 50. God is compassionate and desires to help.
  C. His strength is revealed in verses 51 and 52. Some may have a desire to help without the power to do so.
    1. Mary reminds all of us of the mighty strength of God, who not only wants to help but also has the ability to do whatever needs to be done to accomplish His purpose.
    2. Illustration: He had the power to part the Red Sea because His purpose was deliverance for His people.
  D. His faithfulness is found in verses 53-55.
    1. God has never failed His people, nor will He ever fail them.
    2. His record of faithfulness is perfect.

## Conclusion

What song will you sing this Christmas? You could sing a song of despair, defeat, and gloom from the domination of the circumstances that surround you.

Or you can rise up on wings of faith and confidence in God and sing the songs of praise that come gushing forth from the heart of one who has learned to believe God and trust Him in all things.

## Close with a Carol

"Joy to the World"

# ZECHARIAH'S SONG OF PRAISE

## Luke 1:67-79

**Introduction**
- A. Last Sunday we looked at Mary's song of pure joy.
    1. It was a song of joy realized because God's promises were being fulfilled.
    2. It was a song of praise because of the qualities that Mary saw in God.
- B. On this second Sunday we look at Zechariah's song of praise. Read the scripture, 1:67-79.
    1. Who is Zechariah?
        - *a.* He was the father of John the Baptist, who introduced Jesus.
        - *b.* He was a priest, a descendant of Aaron.
    2. Zechariah's story and song point out seven steps by which we can increase our awareness of God and thereby fully enjoy our daily lives.

## I. The First Step Is to Take God Seriously (vv. 5-7)
- A. Zechariah and Elizabeth intentionally looked to God and waited to know His will.
    1. Look at verse 6. What a great compliment!
    2. In spite of their affliction in not having children, they still maintained a positive attitude toward God.
- B. We need to give serious consideration to the reality of God and His will for our lives.

## II. The Second Step Is to Serve the Lord (vv. 8-10)
- A. Zechariah was faithful in his pursuit of service to God.
- B. Those who find some way of ministering before the Lord discover that this draws them closer to God.

## III. The Third Step Is to Make Prayer a Daily Part of Life (vv. 11-17)
- A. Gabriel appeared to Zechariah during his time of prayer.
- B. God reveals himself to people who take Him seriously.

## IV. The Fourth Step Is to Believe God's Word (vv. 18-22)

A. Zechariah's doubt caused a temporary communication problem.

B. God gave him a reason to move his confidence beyond lip service.

C. We can never get close to God until we live as though we believe the Bible.

## V. The Fifth Step Is to Give God Praise for Victory (vv. 23-25)

A. Elizabeth became pregnant and gave God the credit.

B. She acknowledged the miracle that was taking place in her life.

## VI. The Sixth Step Is to Obey God When All Is Going Well (vv. 57-66)

A. They were living in parental poverty until God blessed them with their son, John.

B. It is easy to forget God when all is going well.

## VII. The Seventh Step Is to Fix Your Heart on God (vv. 67-79)

A. Zechariah's song is like an Old Testament psalm.

B. He understood that without God's kindness he would be the victim of his childless situation.

C. Zechariah demonstrated a proper sense of priorities.

D. It is a blessing to trust God for the way He provides for every area in our lives.

## Conclusion

A. This a good time to draw closer to God.

B. If you can hear what Zechariah is singing and follow his example, this will be a great time of joy and praise.

C. For those who follow the example of Zechariah, Christmas will be a time of great joy and growing close to God.

## Close with a Carol

"Hark! the Herald Angels Sing"

11

# THE ANGELS' SONG OF GOOD NEWS

## Luke 2:8-20

### Introduction

A. We are considering the songs of Christmas. Mary's song was about the pure joy of total commitment. Zechariah's song was about the praise that comes from taking God seriously.

B. Today we are going to look at the song of the angels.

C. Read the song, Luke 2:8-20.

### I. The Song Was First Sung to Shepherds

A. Why did God choose shepherds?

1. Shepherds represent the forgotten people of the world. While God sent a star to the magi, the stars put shepherds to sleep at night. So God gave them an angel chorus.

2. God sends the message to each of us in a way that we can understand.

B. The message is good news.

1. The Scriptures had promised that God would be with us (Isa. 7:14). The angels are saying, "He is here."

2. The Scriptures had promised that light would come. They would have a Counselor and Prince of Peace (9:2-6). The angels are saying, "He is here."

3. The Scriptures had promised that someday they would experience the Lord's favor (61:1-3). The angels are saying, "This is the day."

4. This is good news that brings joy to the hearts of all of God's people. All of those things the angel chorus announced are still in force.

### II. The Message of the Song That the Angels Sang

A. The message of this song is for each one and for everyone.

1. The significance of each one means that God does not consider us as a crowd of people. He sees each of us individually.
2. The message is all-inclusive. No one is to be left out of what God is doing. The announcement was as broad as the human race and as enduring as time.

B. The message of this song is that the Savior has come.
1. "Savior" is a favorite term used by both Luke and Paul. They use it over 40 times.
2. "Savior" literally means "the one to make safe, to preserve, or to make alive."
3. The angels are saying, "The One who will provide eternal life is here."

C. The song assured them that they could find Him (Luke 2:12).

D. The song told the shepherds how to recognize Him (v. 12).

## III. The Result of Listening to the Angels' Song Is Great Joy (vv. 15-20)

A. There was not much joy in the life of a shepherd.
1. They lived in poverty and loneliness.
2. Because they were wise enough to follow the guidance God gave them, they found great joy.

B. This discovery is still being made today. Those who listen to what God is saying and follow His direction find reason to experience great joy.

## Conclusion

A. Mary found joy. Zechariah found joy. The shepherds found joy.

B. In each instance, those who found a reason to rejoice listened to God and submitted their wills to Him.
   —*What about you?*

C. The angels sang a song of good news. The shepherds discovered its meaning because they listened and followed the tug at their hearts.
   —*Will you?*

## Close with a Carol

"Silent Night! Holy Night!"

# SIMEON'S SONG OF RECOGNITION

## Luke 2:21-35

### Introduction

A. We have looked at three of the scriptural songs of Christmas.
  1. Mary's song of praise that is the result of total commitment to God's will
  2. Zechariah's song of joy that is the result of taking God at His word
  3. The angels' song of good news that brings hope, joy, and gladness
B. This week we are looking at the last Christmas song—Simeon's song of recognition of the advent of the Savior.
C. Read the scripture, Luke 2:21-35.

### I. God Speaks to People Who Are Listening to Him (vv. 25-26)

A. There are four key thoughts in this passage.
  1. Simeon was faithful in waiting for God's message.
  2. It is encouraging to note that at a time of apostasy among the priesthood, God still had some priests who were faithful.
  3. Simeon was anticipating God's work in the deliverance of Israel.
  4. God was revealing to Simeon what he had been anticipating.
B. Throughout history those who were listening for God heard Him—Noah, Moses, Zechariah.
C. Those who are listening to God will hear His voice when the time is right (vv. 27-30).
D. This lesson is still good. God's promise in Prov. 3:5-6 is still good.

### II. Those Who Believe God and Live like It Receive Special Blessings

14

A. It is one thing to be given guidance. It is something else to respond positively.
   1. In Luke 2:29-32 Simeon says, "You promised. I received." His words communicate no holding back.
   2. He was giving more than lip service to his profession of faith in God.
B. It was the same way with the other people of the Christmas story.
   1. Mary became the mother of Christ because she believed God (1:38).
   2. Joseph became the Master's earthly father because he refused to divorce Mary (Matt. 1:20-25).
   3. Zechariah spoke again because he obeyed God in naming his son (Luke 1:63-64).
   4. The shepherds found great joy because they acted as a result of their belief (2:15-20).

## III. When God Blesses Our Lives, We Need to Respond with Praise

A. Simeon had been waiting for God to send the Savior (vv. 25-35).
   1. He was "waiting on God" is a brief summary of Simeon's life.
   2. When God responded to Simeon's faith, he openly expressed his joy.
B. Anna responded the same way. Note verses 36-38.
   1. She was firm in her open recognition of Jesus as the Promised One.
   2. One of the reasons so many miss joy is because they are hesitant to acknowledge Jesus as Lord. They are afraid they might be wrong.
C. Those who truly know the joy of Jesus are those who live openly in their commitment to Him. Fearful Christians live miserable lives. Open confidence brings respect and joy.

## Conclusion

The song of Simeon says: (1) Jesus is for real; (2) openly acknowledge Him; and (3) enjoy life because you have found the answer others are still seeking.

## Close with a Song

"Joyful, Joyful, We Adore You"

# Part II

# MESSAGES ON THE COMING OF GOD

This series of messages was prepared to help create a sense of anticipation for the Christmas season. The first two messages will help the listener understand that the Christmas story is not confined to Matt. 1—2 or to Luke 1—2. There is much more to the story, and even the message that follows Christmas Sunday helps us rejoice in the fact that God wrapped himself in flesh and came into our world.

# The Coming of God—Message One

## John 1:1-14

**Introduction**
- A. Christmas means many things to many people. For some it means giving and receiving gifts; for some, parties and celebrations; for others, traditions rich in meaning. But the reason we celebrate is that God came to earth.
- B. We are endeavoring in this series of messages to make Christmas a season.
  1. While it will be climaxed by one day, we will not limit it to just that day.
  2. There are many things that will steal the beauty of Christmas if we let them.
  3. The biggest theft of all will be the taking away of spiritual growth by secular pressure.
- C. Careful attention to John's message will enable us to make the most of our opportunity for growth in God.

## I. Why Did God Come?
- A. Who could ever understand why He came?
  1. It had to be for love alone.
  2. When we look at the universe, we are forced to wonder why He came to earth.
  3. In comparison with what He had left, what would He have lost if He had abandoned the world as we know it?
- B. God came because He loves humankind.

## II. God Had Promised to Rescue Humankind
- A. "And I will put enmity between you and the woman, and between your offspring and hers; he will crush your head, and you will strike his heel" (Gen. 3:15).
- B. According to the King James Version, "The sceptre shall not depart from Judah, nor a lawgiver from between his feet, until Shiloh come; and unto him shall the gathering of the people be" (49:10).

C. According to Isa. 7:1-14, deliverance will come to God's people.

## III. In John 1:1,14 His Coming Is Described

A. It is significant that John recognized Jesus as the Word.
  1. The Word is God's personal expression of himself to humankind.
  2. Jesus said in 14:9, "Anyone who has seen me has seen the Father."
B. The *Amplified Bible* translates 1:14 to read, God "tabernacled among us." "Tabernacled" means He put His tent down beside our tent.

## IV. John Describes Jesus in Verse 16

A. Jesus is the embodiment of grace—God's unmerited favor made available to us.
B. Jesus is truth personified. Truth is the opposite side of the coin of grace. Truth says the requirements of God will not be lowered.
C. There are two distinct sides of Christ.
  1. There is the tender side of grace that reaches to all.
  2. There is the stern side of grace to proud, self-righteous people who do not think they need Him.
D. Before Christ's baptism John left no question in the minds of those who listened. This is God come to earth (see v. 29).

## Conclusion

A. A lesson in English grammar will help us.
  1. If we were to conjugate the past, present, and future of what John is saying, it would be something like this: God came (past); God comes (present); God will come (future).
  2. All are present in this passage: God was here (past); God is here (present); God will be here (future).
  3. Where is here? Wherever you and I are.
B. The coming of God is the most significant event in the world's history. I hope we can grasp its greatness.

## Close with a Carol

"O Come, Let Us Adore Him" (chorus)

# The Coming of God—Message Two

## Isaiah 40:1-12, 28-31

### Introduction
A. Last week we faced the coming of God as described in John 1. He came and made His home beside us. He came because He loves us. He came to have close fellowship with us. He came centuries ago but comes anew every day and will be here with us tomorrow.

B. Since God came to be our neighbor, what is He like? Isa. 40 tells us much about the nature of God.

C. In this chapter there are four significant qualities of our neighbor God. He is mighty (v. 10), He is tender (v. 11), He is permanent (v. 28), and He brings life triumphant (vv. 30-31).

D. He is the kind of neighbor one enjoys. Illustration: Tell about a kind act of a neighbor.

### I. He Is Mighty (vv. 10 and 12)
A. Various translations can help us understand this.
   1. The *Amplified* reads, "With might . . . "
   2. The *American Standard Version* reads, "As a mighty one . . ."
   3. *The Living Bible* reads, "With mighty power; . . . with awesome strength . . ."
   4. He is describing something so great that the exhibition of its power overwhelms us.

B. The power of God goes beyond our wildest imaginations.
   1. He held the sun still (Josh. 10).
   2. He sealed the heavens for several years and then opened them again (1 Kings 17).

C. How big is God?
   1. "Who else has held the oceans in his hands and measured off the heavens with his ruler? Who else knows the weight of all the earth and weighs the mountains and the hills?" (Isa. 40:12, TLB).

2. The more we learn about our universe, the bigger God becomes.

## II. He Is Tender (v. 11)

A. While God is mighty beyond comparison, He is as tender as a newborn baby. There is no more sensitive picture of God than the one expressed in verse 11. Illustration: Describe the picture of Christ carrying a lamb in His arms.

B. The word picture in 53:2 is different but illustrates the same truth. As the first shoot of life that comes forth from a seed is tender, so is God. His love for us so tenderized our hearts that He feels our slightest touch.

## III. He Is Permanent (40:28)

A. This picture of a powerful but tender God who loves us and wants to live with us is almost more than we can comprehend. He will always be with us.

B. I can count on God. All that He is today He will be tomorrow. The phrase "He will not grow tired or weary" is significant in its encouragement.

## IV. He Is Life Triumphant (vv. 30-31)

A. Life can become exhausting unless we know Him. Read verse 30. Those who depend upon their physical strength will find it eventually leaves them. Those who depend upon God for their strength find renewal for life's journey (v. 31).

B. In chapter 53 He brings healing. In verse 4 we read about the steps He took to bring us spiritual healing. In verse 5 we read the description of what He endured for our healing. We find spiritual victory in the God who came.

## Conclusion

The God who came is mighty, tender, and permanent. He came into our world and took upon himself that punishment we rightfully deserve so we could live victoriously. Is it any wonder that Isaiah cries in 40:1, "Comfort, comfort my people, says your God."

## Close with a Carol

"Hark! the Herald Angels Sing"

# The Coming of God—Message Three

## Luke 2:1-20

**Introduction**
    A. We have been anticipating this day. We looked at His coming as described in John 1. God was so motivated by love that He came to dwell with us. In Isa. 40 we looked at the nature of the God who came.
    B. The picture is ready to be completed—God has come.
       1. Luke describes His coming in a beautiful, tender way.
       2. Today we will look at the message of the angels.

**I. The Angels Announced That All Fear Is Gone (v. 10)**
    A. The shepherds were told not to be afraid of the situation in which they found themselves.
    B. The message also promised the removal of fear in the future.
       1. Most fear comes from a feeling of uncertainty. There is no uncertainty with Jesus.
       2. The Jews wondered if God had forgotten them. The message is, "Fear not. God has not forgotten you—He will never forget you."
       3. Sometimes an uncertain future can be a frightening experience.
       4. The prospects of failure can create fear in our hearts.
       —He who can do anything has come. Therefore, in Him I can do all things.
       5. Some people are afraid of eternity.
       —Because God came, death is merely our door of access to a glorious eternity with Him in heaven.
    C. Now we understand why the words "Fear not—now or ever" are so significant.

**II. The Angels Announced That Great Joy Has Come (v. 10)**
    A. The Greek word for great is *mega*.
       1. We understand that *mega* means something of enor-

21

mous size. The angels are saying, then, that the greatest joy imaginable is here.

2. The absence of fear is one thing. But the presence of joy is something else.

B. The angels were excited about the news they were announcing.

C. "Megajoy" is still available to those who are listening. Joy belongs to those who take a trip to the manger and bow before God wrapped in flesh.

## III. The Angels Announced That the Savior Is Here (v. 11)

A. The message is a personal one—"Unto *you*" (KJV, emphasis added).

B. The angelic messengers could have used other words.
1. There had been no voice for 400 years.
2. A prophet such as Elijah or Isaiah would have been welcomed. But they needed more. They needed a Savior.
3. A teacher or rabbi would have been welcomed. Jesus was that—and more.
4. A new leader like Joshua or Moses would have been helpful. Jesus is the ultimate Deliverer—setting all who believe in Him free from the slavery of sin.
5. They needed more than any man could provide. They needed *God*—a Savior.

C. The word "savior" is significant.
1. The word means "to make safe, to deliver, to preserve, to make alive."
2. All of this definition is found in Jesus. He makes us safe. He delivers us from sin, He preserves our lives (John 3:16), and He makes us fully alive.

## Conclusion

The Jews had anticipated what we know in full. Away with fear—Jesus is born! Joy to the world—Jesus is born! The Savior has come—Jesus is born! The birth of Jesus is the greatest event since God said, "Let there be light."

## Close with a Carol

"Joy to the World"

# The Coming of God—Message Four

## Matthew 2:1-12

### Introduction
  A. The announcement of the coming of God has been made.
    1. Communication is a peculiar thing in that people react differently to the same set of words.
    2. This is the way it was when Jesus was born. Some people were upset. Some people were oblivious. Some people were thrilled with the message.
  B. These same reactions to the Christmas story still take place. The question is not "Will I react?" but "How will I react?"
  C. We will consider reactions that followed the coming of God on that first Advent.
  D. Read the scripture, Matt. 2:1-12.

### I. Herod Was Disturbed (v. 3)
  A. Why did the message bother Herod so much?
    1. He was concerned that nothing would disturb his self-centered, self-controlled life.
    2. If the story of the wise men proved to be true, Herod had a rival to his throne.
    3. One fact should not go unnoticed—verse 3*b:* "All Jerusalem [was disturbed] with him." The population had adjusted to Herod's rules and did not want to change.
  B. The coming of God in the form of Christ still disturbs people today.
    1. Some people almost violently oppose any sign that the message might be true.
    2. Try as they may, no one can destroy the Christmas story any more than Herod could destroy the young Baby.

## II. The Innkeeper Missed the Beauty of the First Advent (Luke 2:7)

A. Since every inn has a keeper, someone missed a great opportunity.
   1. He was there and had a chance to be in on the world's greatest event but missed it.
   2. The King of Kings was on his doorstep, but he had no place for Him.
B. There are many innkeepers in our world. To them the story of Christmas represents money, gifts, and parties. They don't oppose the message. In their busyness they just miss it.

## III. Some People Discover the Beauty of the Coming of God

A. Mary discovered the beauty of being God's vessel (Luke 1:46-47). To Mary the Christmas story means the thrill of being used by God. Mary was drawn closer to God by the message of Christmas (v. 38).
B. The angels rejoiced at the privilege of carrying the message.
   1. It was not a duty to go to the hillside and proclaim the good news (2:13-14).
   2. Christians today are thrilled with the message of Christmas. It makes it easy to tell the story.
C. Shepherds believed the message and confirmed it in their lives (v. 20).
   1. These men had a personal experience with the manger Child.
   2. We, too, can have a special experience at Christmas by taking advantage of the invitation to draw close to Him.

## Conclusion

While the season of Christmas has passed, our reaction to the message has just begun. Each of us fits into the Christmas story in some way. We can choose to be angry as Herod was, ignore it as the innkeeper did, or experience "joy unspeakable and full of glory" as Mary and the angels had. What will be your response?

## Close with a Carol

"O Come, All Ye Faithful"

# Part III
# Messages on the Promise

The first three weeks of this series of messages are focused on prophetic passages that promise the birth of Jesus. We will be taking brief looks at segments of scriptures concerning God's promises to send us a Messiah. Week four points out the fulfillment of God's promises. Week five asks a very pointed question about our response to God's keeping of His promises.

# THE PROMISE—MESSAGE ONE

## Isaiah 7 and 9

### Introduction

A. Christmas began in the Garden of Eden. Adam and Eve had a very good life going—no pain, no toil, no heartache. Satan, through his crafty lies, destroyed that perfect existence and tricked Adam into breaking his relationship with God.

B. God could have abandoned the Adam-Eve project. Who would have blamed God, since humankind had become such a problem? God had invested too much of himself in humankind to abandon the highest order of creation. He promised to provide humankind with the help needed to return to the relationship Adam and Eve had enjoyed before the Fall.

C. Read the scripture, Isa. 7:11-14 and 9:1-6.

D. God will keep His promises. He has kept every promise He ever made to humankind. We will be considering some of His promises and the fulfillment of them through Jesus. We will begin by looking at the first promise that God made in the Garden of Eden.

### I. The Need for a Deliverer Is First Evidenced in the Garden of Eden

A. In Gen. 3:15 God promises victory in the struggle.

B. We will not take time to discuss the Fall at length. It is sufficient to say that Satan was smarter than humankind. Everyone who has ever matched wits with Satan has been a loser.

C. God promised a Deliverer (v. 15). In this verse God is promising to destroy the dominance of sin over humanity. And He did through Jesus.

D. Christmas is the fulfillment of God's promise to provide the life He had planned for His highest creation.

## II. The Need for Deliverance Continued to Be Exhibited in Isa. 7

A. The problem that elicited the promise of Isa. 7 was serious.
  1. God's people were being threatened by their fellows.
  2. Verses 5-9 describe how the scheming neighbors wanted to inflict their heathen lifestyle on Israel. There is still a war going on, and we are caught in the struggle.
  3. God promises a Deliverer in verse 14. King Ahaz had difficulty in believing that God would intervene. He refused to accept the promise and paid a terrible price for aligning himself with the king of Assyria (2 Kings 16:7).
  4. We have the option of believing God and having Him with us (Immanuel) or of failing to believe and having Him against us.
B. The promise in Isa. 9 is for help with the affairs of our lives.
  1. In verse 1 the promise is "no more gloom for those who were in distress." Help is available. So there is no reason to be downcast. We will not be distressed if we ask God to give us guidance.
  2. In verse 6 there is encouragement for our daily lives.
    *a.* The "Wonderful Counselor" will give us the advice we need to make the right decisions for our lives. Our mighty God gives us power for every problem we face.
    *b.* Our Everlasting Father will never pass away or leave us. The Prince of Peace means not only the absence of war but also a condition of rich, harmonious, and positive well-being.
  3. What a beautiful promise God has given to His people!

## Conclusion

The record is clear. What God promises, He provides. Christmas is our celebration of His keeping His promise to the world.

## Close with a Carol

"It Came upon the Midnight Clear"

# The Promise—Message Two

## Isaiah 40 and 55

### Introduction

A. Last week we began to look at the promise of Jesus' coming.
  1. We studied the promise of God's absolute domination of Satan in Gen. 3.
  2. We looked at the promise of a Deliverer who would come according to Isa. 7. He would come through a virgin and would be Immanuel, God with us. Therefore, wherever believers are, God is present with them.
  3. We looked in Isa. 9 at the promise to deliver us from gloom and darkness and to give us help in our daily lives.

B. Today we are going to look at another area of promise from Isa. 40 and 55.

C. Read the scripture, Isa. 40:1-5, 9-11, 28-31.

### I. The Promise of Comfort in Time of Need (Isa. 40)

A. Did Jesus fulfill this promise of comfort?
  1. Ask Jairus, whose daughter was brought back to life (Mark 5:22-43).
  2. Ask the lepers who had been banished from their families (Luke 17:11-19).
  3. Ask the man who had spent 38 years by the pool of Bethesda (John 5:1-15).
  4. He still brings comfort to those whose hearts are broken.

B. In Isa. 40:11 we are given the promise of an intimate relationship with God.
  1. A shepherd has a very special tender relationship with his sheep.
    —Illustration: Describe a shepherd who is reaching out to a sheep that is in need.
  2. Isaiah presents two clear pictures. In verse 10 God is a strong conqueror subduing all resistance. In verse 11

He is a tender, compassionate shepherd who is caring for newborn lambs who are too weak to travel.

C. The promise is that He will never get weary (v. 28). We sometimes grow weary emotionally and physically. God never does. He is always fresh. In verse 31 those who look to Jesus in faith will find a renewal of their strength.

## II. In Isa. 55:1-13 We Are Given the Promise of a Full Life

A. Many people live on the dregs of life.
   1. They have an abundance of the stuff of the world but no deep, internal satisfaction.
   2. Illustration: Many celebrities have everything the world can give but nothing that satisfies their souls.
B. God has a wonderful life planned for His people.
   1. A life centered in Jesus is the best one available.
   2. Christians may not have an abundance of material possessions, but we have an abundance of life.
C. To receive the full meaning of this promise, we need to tie together chapters 53, 54, and 55. In chapter 53 the promise is for redemption. In chapter 54 the promise is for a fulfilled life. In chapter 55 the promise is for a life of abundance of the things that matter most.
D. The offer in chapter 55 is very clear. Verse 1 invites us to come to the Lord. Verse 6 urges us to seek the Lord. Verse 7 offers forgiveness for our sins. Verse 12 promises the pure joy found by those who follow these steps.

## Conclusion

A. The promise of life as it was meant to be is ours for the taking.
   —Illustration: Describe scenes at your house on Christmas morning. When does a gift become yours? Not until you take it and open it.
B. God is pleased when we take His promise at face value and make it our own.

## Close with a Carol

"What Child Is This?"

# THE PROMISE—MESSAGE THREE

## Matthew 1:18-23

**Introduction**

A. There is a phrase that we hear often in the Christmas story. It is, "that it might be fulfilled which was spoken . . . by the prophet" (KJV). This is our text for today. Read the scripture, Matt. 1:18-23. Also, call attention to 2:5, 15, and 17.

B. Prophecy of the coming Messiah began early in the story of God and humankind. Most people consider Gen. 3:15 the first of those prophetic utterances.

C. What is prophecy? A prophecy is a promise from God that something is going to happen. In the case of the messianic prophecies, God was promising His people that He had not forgotten them nor would He ever forget them.

D. The prophecy that began in Genesis weaves its way through the entire Book of God. It built a strong sense of expectancy and hope in those who heard the words. A careful consideration of the prophecy will do the same for us today.

E. There are four areas of prophecies. We will take a brief look at them.

## I. How the Messiah Would Come into the World (Isa. 7:14)

A. How was it going to happen? The answer is found in verse 14. We may not understand how a virgin could conceive. In fact, that is what makes Jesus' birth a miracle. Anything less than a miraculous conception by a virgin would eliminate the beautiful truth, "God is with us."

B. It would be necessary for the Messiah to come through the ancestral line of the Hebrews (11:1).

## II. Where the Messiah Would Be Born (Mic. 5:2)

A. Jerusalem was the star city of Israel. It was the capital city and site of the Temple. Everything of importance should have happened there.

B. God would have no part of a caste system. One overwhelming truth of the Christmas story is its strong message that God loves all people everywhere.

C. Micah was a minor prophet with a major promise (v. 2). Bethlehem means "House of Bread." To this city God sent the Bread of Life (John 6:35, 41, 48).

D. God promised the staff of life to all people by choosing Bethlehem as the location for His Son's birth.

## III. What Was the Messiah to Be Like? (Isa. 9)

A. The coming of One as powerful as the Messiah could have been frightening. While He would deliver them from their enemies, He could have also dominated their lives as some kings had done.

B. God promised He would be sensitive to all people (v. 6).

1. He is a "Wonderful Counselor." A wonderful Counselor is someone who understands people and has a genuine interest in giving them good advice. This is Jesus.

2. He is a "Mighty God." This means that He is One who is in the position to make a difference whenever there is a need. This is Jesus.

3. The "Everlasting Father" means He is eternal. This is Jesus.

4. The "Prince of Peace" is One who has the ability to impart calmness in the midst of turbulent situations. This is Jesus.

## IV. The Result of His Coming Is Foretold in Isa. 53 and 55

A. God promised He would meet humankind's deepest needs (53:4-6).

B. With this forgiveness, chapter 55 becomes a reality and our souls become fully alive (vv. 1-3).

## Conclusion:

The prophecies are promises from God. Looking back, we see all of the prophecies fulfilled in Jesus. Looking forward, the prophecies help us to anticipate the real beauty of Christmas.

## Close with a Carol

"O Come, O Come, Emmanuel"

# The Promise Fulfilled

## Luke 2

### Introduction

A. We have been looking at the promise of a Messiah.
   1. God's promise was for a Messiah who would lead His people to a better life than they had ever experienced.
   2. For many years they held tightly to the hope the promise offered.
B. God always keeps His promises to His people.
   1. Sometimes the promises were made and fulfilled in the face of seemingly impossible situations.
   2. His greatest promise was that a Messiah would come despite the extraordinary means that would be required to bring fulfillment.
C. There were times when the people must have wondered if this was the one promise that would never be fulfilled. 400 years is a long time to wait without fulfillment or even a word of encouragement or hope.
D. Finally, God said, "The hour has come" (see Gal. 4:4). In one mighty, miraculous act God swept away the many years of emptiness and frustration.
E. God kept His word. The promise is fulfilled. Read Luke 2:1-20.

## I. It Is a Personal Message—"Unto You" (v. 11)

A. The message is universal in its scope. All classes of people are involved from poor shepherds to rich kings. When the angel said "all the people" in verse 10, that meant anyone and everyone.
B. It is personal in its application "to you." The message from God is given to you personally. You can do with the message whatever you wish—lose it among the rubble of a secular Christmas or hold it in the beauty of its significance.

## II. It Is a Present-Day Message (v. 11)

A. The fact that it is present adds great significance in a wonderful way. "Has been born" in the NIV literally means "no more looking, hoping, waiting." The Jews had been anticipating this event that has now come to pass.

B. The promise was not just for ancient believers but for present people as well. My Messiah is here. I do not need to wait for His coming. Great news—whatever He was, He still is and always will be (Heb. 13:8).

## III. It Is a Precious Message—"The Savior Has Come"

A. The name Jesus compares to the ancient Hebrew name Joshua. Jesus is to us what Joshua was to the Jews of old. Moses led the children out of Egypt, but Joshua led them into Canaan. Jesus keeps us from wandering aimlessly through life.

B. The message of Christmas speaks to humankind's deepest needs. Of all of the things we need in life, forgiveness from sins is our most pressing one (Rom. 3:23). Jesus brings peace to those who accept Him.

## Conclusion

A. There will be promises under each of our Christmas trees. We call them presents. But they are only a promise until we take them in faith and open them. They become our personal possessions when we take hold of them in the spirit in which they were given.

B. God's promises are ours for the taking. Peace, power, and victory over Satan and surroundings have been wrapped in love and placed at our disposal. Take God's gift. Make it your own. And let the promise be fulfilled in your life. Angelus Silesius has said:

> Tho Christ a thousand times
> In Bethlehem be born,
> If He's not born in thee
> Thy soul is still forlorn.

## Close with a Carol

"Joy to the World"

33

# THE RESULTS OF THE PROMISE IN OUR WORLD

## Matthew 1:18-25

**Introduction**
- A. If God was looking for a home into which His Son could come, would He choose yours?
- B. Is there enough love in your home?
- C. Is there enough commitment to God in your home?
- D. Does your home have the godly atmosphere of the following? A healthy relationship with others. Personal discipline in things that matter most. Keeping of your vows to God, including your marriage vows.
- E. Read the scripture, Matt. 1:18-25.
- F. Would your home meet His requirements for an earthly dwelling for His Son? Let's look at the qualities that made Mary and Joseph's the ideal residence for God to use to fulfill His promise.

## I. God Will Use a Home Filled with Love (v. 19)
- A. Matthew clearly speaks of Joseph's love for Mary. Love covers all faults. Joseph loved Mary in spite of what he perceived to be her faults.
- B. Love does not demand its own way.
- C. Love understands extenuating circumstances and makes allowances for them.
- D. Love forgives and carries no grudges. Therefore, the abrasions and hurts that we inflict upon each other can heal.
- E. Is there enough love in your home to offset whatever problems the hazards of marriage raise?

## II. God Will Use a Home Filled with Commitment
- A. Mary's commitment to God is described in Luke 1:38.
- B. Joseph's commitment to God is described in Matt 1:20-24.

C. Their joint commitment to God is described in Luke 2:41-42.
D. What is the level of commitment to God in your home?
   1. Do the things of God take precedence over secular things?
   2. Do your children have good cause to believe God is first in your life? Your children are more perceptive of your attitude toward God than you may realize.

## III. God Will Use a Home That Has a Healthy Atmosphere

A. In order to have a God-blessed home, we must have a healthy attitude toward others.
   1. A caring attitude toward your spouse and children is essential. A respectful attitude toward the people with whom you worship is essential. A respectful attitude toward neighbors and fellow workers is an absolute requirement.
   2. God's Son loves, respects, and cares for everyone. Do you communicate these qualities to those around you?
B. Is there an atmosphere of personal discipline present in your home?
   1. In order to withstand the pressures He would face, God's Son would need a disciplined life.
   2. Our personal habits will make us stronger or weaker in the faith.
   3. Sloppy habits lead to sloppy living.
C. When the atmosphere in our home exhibits the keeping of our vows to God, the promise will be fulfilled within our family.

## Conclusion

A. All things considered, when the promise is fulfilled, a dramatic demonstration of God's special plan is revealed.
B. God is looking for places to fulfill His promise of revealing His love to the world. Do you need to do some housework to get ready for Him?

## Close with a Song

"Let the Beauty of Jesus Be Seen in Me"

# Part IV

# MESSAGES ON THE OPPORTUNITIES CHRISTMAS OFFERS

This series of messages emphasizes some of the opportunities of Christmas that often get overlooked. While the scripture may be familiar, the opportunities that grow out of Christmas are sometimes lost in the activities surrounding the season. The moments to strengthen family ties or to focus on the divinity of Jesus are often missed. Emphasis on the excitement of Christmas is given many times, but what happened beyond Bethlehem can go unnoticed. These messages give a congregation the privilege to look at some facets of the Christmas story that are often missed.

# CHRISTMAS IS A FAMILY AFFAIR

## Hebrews 11:1-7

### Introduction

A. This may seem like a strange text for Christmas, and it may very well be. Still, it is not irrelevant to the beautiful story of Christ's birth and its deepest meaning.

B. There is a crying need to develop and strengthen our homes. In all too many situations we have gotten so caught up in the affairs of life that we have forgotten how to live. As we have done this, we have paid for it with weakened families.

C. Many lovely houses have no families in them—only people.

    1. Illustration: The story is told of a little boy who when asked where he lived responded, "We have no house." When the questioner expressed concern that he had no home, the little boy replied, "We have a home, but we just don't have a house to put it in." It is better to have a home without a house than to have a house without a home.

    2. The scripture tells us of a man who by his faith in God was able to save his family. Let's consider together Christmas as a family affair.

### I. The Story of Noah

A. How does this lend its influence to the subject for today? Buried in this scripture is a phrase we could easily miss: "[He] built an ark to save his family" (v. 7). The story of Noah is one of a man whose faith in and obedience to God resulted in rescuing his family from destruction.

B. As we consider the story of Noah, there are striking similarities to our day. According to Gen. 6:5, there was no spiritual awareness. They were continuously seeking new ways to satisfy the flesh. According to verse 11, crime abounded everywhere and violence was the order of the day. Noah and his family were in the minority.

C. Although Noah was in the minority, he was in tune with God. He "walked with God" (v. 9).
  1. Because of his walk, God gave him instructions on how to save his family from the coming destruction.
  2. The people of his day must have thought Noah was crazy. He was building an ark in the desert for something that had never happened before—a flood. Noah's children may have wondered if their dad had gone off the deep end. There was something, however, in his life that caused them to have confidence in him.
  3. According to 7:11-23, when the critical hour came, Noah's family was saved because of their confidence in his faith.

## II. Christmas Is a Family Affair

A. In strengthening family relationships under God's guidance, someone will have to take the lead to build an "ark."
B. The first Christmas was a family affair. A mother and father who had faith in God risked ridicule, and God gave them a home like no other that has ever existed. If anything beautiful happens in your home, Mom and Dad will need to take the lead. Children can cause some things to happen, but the real beauty of Christmas is when the whole group makes it a family affair.
C. Christmas is a fun time. It is a great time to do things together as a family. Family time activities are endless—activities around the Christmas tree, special events at church, and so on. Christmas is a time for establishing and maintaining family traditions.

## Conclusion

A. Those families that take advantage of the opportunities of Christmas will find their homes to be as safe as the ark.
B. Give your family a priceless gift this year. Give them yourself, and make this Christmas a family affair. Put a home in your house.

## Close with a Carol

"Hark! the Herald Angels Sing"

# CHRISTMAS IS A DIVINE AFFAIR

## John 1:1-14

**Introduction**

   A. Last week we looked at Christmas as a family affair. I hope you are remembering how vital this is and that you are taking advantage of it.

      1. Be sure to let nothing keep you from having some family times together.

      2. There is always time for the "most important things," and family involvements are critical.

   B. This week want to take another look at the Christmas story.

      1. Without the divinity of Jesus Christ, Christmas is no different than any other holiday.

      2. Some people do not believe in the Virgin Birth and divine nature, but the Bible clearly teaches these truths.

      3. The virgin birth of Jesus is necessary for the divine nature. This is clearly at the heart of the gospel.

   C. Read the scripture, John 1:1-14.

**I. The Bible Promises a Divine Involvement in Christmas**

   A. Isa. 7:14 is clearly a promise of a divine nature.

      1. The miraculous conception would provide Mary's Child with that nature.

      2. Matthew understood this prophecy to apply to Jesus and make Him divine (Matt. 1:22-23).

   B. Isa. 9:6 promises One who will be a "Mighty God."

      1. John 1:1 points to the fulfillment of this prophecy in the coming of Jesus.

      2. Only One with a divine nature could bring about the miracles that Jesus performed.

   C. The promise to Mary in Luke 1:34-35 was that God was sending a divine Child. While skeptics question Mary's purity, those who have confidence in God's Word accept her testimony.

D. The revelation to Joseph was that a divine experience was to take place (Matt. 1:18-20). God's Word clearly promises that the Child of Christmas would be of divine nature.

## II. The Nature of Jesus Validated the Promise of Divinity

A. Only One of divine nature could bring about the miracles He performed.
   1. Jesus turned water into wine (John 2).
   2. He multiplied bread and fish to feed 5,000 (chap. 6).
   3. Only God could bring the dead to life as He did with Lazarus (chap. 11).
   4. Note: Use other miracles to illustrate this point as appropriate.
   5. The Child born with the promise of a divine nature grew into a Man who exhibited the power of God.

B. The centurion at the Crucifixion testified to the divinity of Christ (Matt. 27:54).
   1. The opinion of this man carries a lot of weight.
   2. He had seen many men die. He saw something different in Jesus.

C. The apostle Paul, a skeptical Pharisee, became a believer after meeting Jesus. Writing to the people of Galatia in Gal. 4:4, Paul said, "When the time had fully come, God sent his Son, born of a woman."

D. The record of history sustains the claim.
   1. No person has ever impacted the world as Jesus has.
   2. No movement in history has been attacked to the extent that Christianity has been.
   3. Remove the influence of Jesus, and all history must be rewritten. It is *His story.*

## Conclusion

It is logical to conclude that although Christmas is fun and has many secular aspects, most important of all, Christmas is a divine affair. If you truly believe this, your Christmas schedule will have time for the One whose birth we celebrate.

## Close with a Carol

"O Little Town of Bethlehem"

# CHRISTMAS IS AN EXCITING AFFAIR

## Luke 2:1-20

**Introduction**
- A. We have been looking at different aspects of the Christmas story as a family affair and as a divine affair. Today we will look at the excitement of Christmas.
- B. There is no time of the year that exudes excitement as much as Christmas. All of the activities of Christmas point to an exciting moment. The music of Christmas is joyful and exciting. The Christmas colors are bright and speak of excitement and life. People in general are lighthearted and upbeat about this holy season.
- C. Read the story of the first Christmas in Luke 2:1-20.

### I. The Incident on the Hillside Was Electrifying
- A. Get the picture of a quiet, calm night that is suddenly transformed by bright lights and great voices. What a way to announce the birth of a Child!
- B. Birth announcements are always exciting.
   1. When Prince Charles of England was born in November 1948, there were 21- and 41-gun salutes as all London celebrated. Most of us don't go that far, but I have seen some announcements on business marquees.
   2. Almost all of us who have had children made excited phone calls and mailed out announcements to our families and friends. We wanted everyone we knew to share our joy—so did God!

### II. The Message of the Angels Was Wonderful
- A. It was a universal message—"unto you" (v. 11, KJV) means "unto everyone."
   1. It was universal in its scope. All classes of people from poor shepherds to rich kings were included.
   2. It was not just for the Jews but also for those of us who are Gentiles.

41

B. While the message was universal, it was also personal.
   1. It is a message from God to you as an individual.
   2. You can do with it whatever you will. You can lose it among the rubble of a secular Christmas or hold on to its beauty and significance.
   3. Somewhere, sometime, make sure to get alone with God and allow this personal message to become yours.
C. It is a present message in that it has happened today (v. 11).
   1. This day is ever present in our lives. Yesterday is gone, tomorrow may not come, but today is here.
   2. To the Jews it meant that the promise long anticipated was now a part of their lives. The fact that Jesus is alive, present and real now, is an exciting truth in our lives.
D. It is a precious message—"a Savior . . . Christ the Lord" (v. 11). We all need a Savior (Rom. 3:23). Jesus gives our lives meaning, direction, satisfaction, and confidence. One of the reasons Christmas is so exciting is because our greatest need has been met.

## Conclusion
A. The shepherds who heard the first Christmas message tested it to make sure it was true (Luke 2:16). They discovered that it was all they had anticipated, and their lives took on more excitement than they had ever experienced (v. 20).
B. Christmas will be exciting for us if we accept its message. If you have grasped the true meaning of this holy season, don't worry about getting the Christmas spirit. It will get you! Take time to do something special with your family. Take a mental journey to the manger and worship the Son of God come to earth. Let your heart rejoice. The greatest news the world has ever heard has come!

## Close with a Carol
"Joy to the World"

# CHRISTMAS IS A LASTING AFFAIR

## Matthew 2:1-12

### Introduction
A. Although Christmas Day is behind us, the purpose of Christmas goes on.
1. The purpose of Christmas was to bring the salvation of humankind. We want that to go on.
2. Today, we are looking at people who came into the Christmas story long after Mary's Baby was delivered in that stable in Bethlehem. Read the scripture, Matt. 2:1-12.
B. We will consider the story of the wise men because they came two years after that Bethlehem night. Christmas did not end with the stable. There are many questions about these people that will never be answered. While tradition and speculation vary, God gave us this story for a reason. He did this to show us how wise men reacted to the message. The Christmas story goes on because the wise still seek Jesus. In that spirit we will take a look at the story of the magi.

### I. These Men Were Wise When They Searched for Jesus
A. The star in the sky was clear for all to see.
1. These men were looking for the greatest truth they could find. Some people never lift their eyes from earthly things long enough to look up.
2. God will only place the star and give its message. It is up to us to recognize the star and its significance.
B. They were wise enough to recognize that the message had special meaning. While they did not know what had happened, they followed the best light they had.
C. They were wise enough to seek the meaning of the special message. What would have happened if they had waited for God to bring the meaning to them? They would have missed the opportunity of a lifetime.

## II. These Men Were Wise When They Worshiped Jesus

A. Everybody does something with Christ. The shepherds and the wise men sought and found Him. Herod and Pilate judged Him and killed Him. The "woman who had lived a sinful life" anointed Him with oil (Luke 7:36-38). What will you do with Jesus?

B. The wise men did not argue with God's highest revelation. They did not try to rationalize and understand. They simply followed God's guidance.

## III. These Men Were Wise When They Gave Jesus the Best They Had

A. Their gifts were symbols of worshiping hearts.
1. They honored God with what He had given to them.
2. Some people think these gifts financed the flight of Mary, Joseph, and Jesus to Egypt (Matt. 2:13-18). In the same way that their gifts were used of God for that sojourn in Egypt, today our gifts enable the message of Jesus to be spread throughout the world.

B. The gifts of the wise men were signs of spontaneous surrender to God.

## IV. They Were Wise When They Refused to Return to Herod

A. They chose not to comply with Herod's request for them to come back to him (v. 8).

B. They trusted God's leadership to the special moment of encounter with Jesus.

C. While we do not know what happened to the wise men, we know why God gave the story to us. It was given to let us know that while wise men followed God's leading then, modern wise men still obey His plan today.

## Conclusion

What guidance is God giving to you? Are you wise enough to follow the star He has given to you?

## Close with a Song

"Where He Leads Me"

# Part V

# LESSONS FROM THE CHRISTMAS STORY

This series of messages will help the listener learn some great lessons from life. As those who listen apply lessons from the Christmas story to their lives, they will experience the real purpose of this holy season, that is, for God and humankind to have a close relationship. This is a five-sermon series. The fifth message should be preached the Sunday following Christmas Day.

# LESSONS FROM THE CHRISTMAS STORY—MESSAGE ONE

## Luke 1

### Introduction

A. There are a number of great lessons to be learned from the Christmas story. As we look at these, we will be able to share the same joy that those involved in the first Nativity experienced.

B. This Christmas season can and will for some people be a time of spiritual growth. No other time of the year directs our attention to so many ordinary people who were wonderfully blessed because they simply listened to God and followed His directions.

C. The lesson for today comes from two very ordinary people who because of their obedience had an extraordinary experience. Read Luke 1:5-20, 57-64.

### I. The Story of the Parents of John the Baptist Is a Great Place to Begin Learning from the Story

A. Zechariah and Elizabeth are two normal people from whom we can learn.

1. They had a serious problem. They were childless. Barrenness was considered a curse in that day. Whose fault was it that they had no children? Someone needed to take the blame, or was that the case?

2. The first lesson is that people who wish to know the joy of God's presence are not focused on fixing blame.

3. In your case the problem may not be to have or not have children, but something just as serious may be causing great distress. The lesson is clear. We have a problem, and we will face it together.

B. They had another problem that was not so serious. But it, too, could create a strained relationship.

1. Zechariah's job required him to be gone for lengthy periods during his term in the Temple.

      2. Their marriage was so healthy that it could weather every situation.

      3. They did not renegotiate their relationship with each stress point that arose.

  C. Many of the problems that come between people would be resolved quickly if they refused to reconsider their commitment.

  D. What has all of this to do with Christmas?

      1. The offer of the choir of angels was "on earth peace among . . . men of good will" (2:14,AMP.).

      2. God's gift of peace and joy to the world is dependent on our ability to remain in love with each other.

## II. The Second Lesson Relates to Blessings That Come from Being Faithful

  A. God blesses those who keep the faith with Him and with each other. Their problem of barrenness was solved (1:11-14). God knew their desires and their problem and saw their faithfulness.

  B. God wants us to have an unshakable faith so that He can help us. Like Zechariah, many of us want a sign or some special assurance (vv. 18-20). Jesus chastised the Pharisees for their desiring a special sign (Matt. 12:39-40).

  C. God keeps His promises (Luke 1:23-24, 57). Zechariah and Elizabeth had learned their lesson. The angel said, "Call him John" (see v. 13). They were obedient to God and were blessed as a result (vv. 59-66).

  D. What kind of child was this? One like Elijah (John 1:21). One who introduced the Messiah (v. 29). One who understood his role in life (3:27-30). One who earned the respect of kings (Matt. 14:1-12).

## Conclusion

The lesson is simple. To know the joy of living to which you are entitled and to experience the peace that Jesus came to give, keep your attitude toward God and humankind right and keep your commitments to whom you have made them.

## Close with a Carol

"O Come, All Ye Faithful"

# Lessons from the Christmas Story—Message Two

## Luke 1

### Introduction

A. Last week's lesson came from Zechariah and Elizabeth. It was the lesson of two ordinary people who learned to handle their problems together. When we keep our promises to God and each other, He provides great joy for our lives regardless of the conditions in which we find ourselves.

B. This week's lesson comes from the scripture that is surrounded by the story of Zechariah and Elizabeth.
   1. Read the scripture, Luke 1:26-55.
   2. The lesson in this passage is simple. Those people wise enough to make a complete commitment to God and keep it enjoy experiences about which the rest of the world can dream.

C. The key to everything in this passage is found in verse 38.
   1. This verse reads, "I am the Lord's servant. May it be to me as you have said."
   2. The lesson we learn from Mary is that pure, unlimited joy is the result of a complete commitment to God's plan.

### I. In Mary's Story We Find Numerous Lessons That Can Enhance Our Personal Lives

A. God honors those who keep His commandments. The commandments call for moral purity. Mary was a virgin (v. 27). In a day of sexual promiscuity it is important to remember God's attitude toward the seventh commandment.

B. We will not always understand what God is doing or how He will do it. Mary was confused, disturbed, even frightened (vv. 29-34). At times we will experience these same emotions. To not understand and to be frightened at the challenges that come our way are not matters of being right or wrong.

48

C. Nothing is impossible with God. What was announced to Mary was impossible under normal, human circumstances. When Mary accepted God's will, it became His responsibility and brought divine ability into the situation.

D. God will help us to understand His leadings. What He asked of Mary was so unusual He decided to help her faith (vv. 36-37). God will clear the matter for you at the necessary time.

## II. Mary's Commitment Was Total (v. 38)

A. In order to experience the joy of God's richest blessings, our response must be an unqualified yes!

B. Mary took a real risk. What would Joseph do? God took care of Joseph (Matt. 1:19-20). Mary could have been stoned to death! There is no way Mary could explain her pregnancy to the people. Illustration: Tell about the woman taken in adultery.

C. Mary laid everything on the line.

## III. The Purest Joy Is Awakened by an Act of Total Commitment

A. Mary experienced the confirmation of God's plan (Luke 1:39-45).

    1. God understands the human side of His creation. He would not leave that dedicated vessel of His to become confused and defeated.

    2. Elizabeth was far enough along in her pregnancy to fit into the divine plan.

B. Unparalleled joy always follows the fulfillment of God's will. In verses 46-55 Mary expresses that joy.

## Conclusion

For two consecutive weeks we have been confronted with a subtle but powerful truth. That truth is that lives of complete commitment to God are honored and blessed by Him. God's gift to you is the ability to be a part of the divine plan and to therefore experience the joy of knowing He is using you. I challenge you. Learn the lesson and the joy of a fully committed life.

## Close with a Carol

"O Little Town of Bethlehem"

# LESSONS FROM THE CHRISTMAS STORY—MESSAGE THREE

## Matthew 2:1-12

### Introduction
Today's lesson comes from another part of the Christmas story. It involves two groups that operate at opposite ends of the social ladder. Each of us fits into one or the other of the brackets formed by shepherds or kings. We will read the scripture from Matt. 2:1-12 but will also refer to Luke 2. Read Matt. 2:1-12.

I. **First, Let's Take a Look at the Lessons from the Shepherds (Luke 2:8-20)**
   A. The shepherds represent the vast majority of humanity.
      1. They were hardworking people who struggled most of their lives to make ends meet.
      2. They were not part of the educated class and had very little power in their world.
      3. They were special to God and had qualities He wanted everyone to experience. They were strong yet tender. They were dependable and committed to their responsibilities.
   B. They listened to God's message (vv. 8-12).
      1. People who are listening will hear God's message of hope (v. 10). Are you tuned into God, or has the static of activities crowded Him out? Illustration: Describe how a radio station broadcasts its message whether we hear it or allow other things to crowd it out.
      2. God deals in light (v. 12). Check it out for yourself.
   C. The shepherds were confirmers (vv. 15-16). Regardless of how good the news may be, it is meaningless to us personally until we confirm it. The promise to the shepherds sounded good, and they discovered that it was. Many times we miss experiencing joy by our failure to "go . . . and see."
   D. The shepherds discovered what others only dreamed of finding (v. 20).

E. The lesson of the shepherds is simple. Those who listen will hear God guiding them to a great discovery of joy and peace. It can only become theirs when it is confirmed.

## II. Second, We Now Look at the Lessons of the Wise Men (Matt. 2:1-12)

A. This lesson is not unlike the shepherds'. However, it does add a new dimension.
   1. Who were these men?
   2. Centuries of study have failed to determine exactly who they were.
   3. We know they were men looking for the highest and best truth that could be found regardless of the effects on their personal lives.
B. They were men who had traveled a great distance.
   1. If the shepherds represent those raised in or near the church, these men represent those with no church background.
   2. All sincere seekers end up at the same place in the presence of Jesus.
   3. All sincere seekers make the same discovery of great joy.
C. These men continued to enjoy the guidance of God.
   1. What happens after we have an encounter with Jesus? (v. 12).
   2. God continues to guide those who would follow His leadership.
D. These men went to great efforts.
   1. Some think they may have traveled two years.
   2. They brought Jesus their very best. Those who will pay the price to follow God's leading come to a "priceless experience."

## Conclusion

We envy the experiences of the shepherds and kings. We can join them if we, too, will follow the leading of our Father.

## Close with a Carol

"O Come, All Ye Faithful"

# Lessons from the Christmas Story—Message Four

## Luke 2:1-20

## Introduction

A. There are many lessons to be learned from the Christmas story.

   1. Since God is sovereign, His will is always accomplished—even a Virgin Birth.

   2. He works through the lives of people who are committed to Him and to their loved ones. Remember the lesson we learned from Elizabeth and Zechariah.

   3. He honors those who keep the commandments and trust Him. Remember the lesson we learned from Mary, the mother of Jesus.

   4. Learners and confirmers experience great joy. Remember the lesson of the shepherds and kings.

B. All of these lessons are important, and yet the greatest lesson of all is the one we come to today.

   God wrapped himself in the form of human flesh and came into our world in order that we might have life. Only love could have motivated God to do that. John 3:16 makes it clear. Read Luke 2:1-20.

## I. Only Love Could Have Motivated God to This Extent

A. Humankind had failed miserably. Humankind failed in the garden. Humankind failed during Noah's time. According to Gen. 11, the Tower of Babel showed humankind's failure in its relationship with God.

B. God chose a nation to glorify Him. Abraham's descendants were to point the minds of the people to Jehovah. The Israelites failed to fulfill their calling. Yet God did not give up.

C. There was nothing about humankind that deserved God's extravagant love. The psalmist asks in Ps. 8:4, "What is man that you are mindful of him?" In Job 7:17 we read, "What is man that you make so much of him, that you give him so much attention . . . ?" We, too, at times feel as though we are miserable failures. Still, He came, and He is here because He loves us.

## II. Love Brought Jesus into Our World

A. The Scriptures are very clear. Paul, speaking of Jesus in Phil. 2:6-8, makes it clear that God's love brought the Christ child to our world. John began his Gospel with the statement that God's love brought His Son into our world.

B. Because of His great love God was not content to give up on the only portion of creation in which He had placed His image. There is something of the divine in each one of us. Of all the myriads of creatures and things, humankind is the highest order.

C. Remember John 3:16. The message of undeserved love is given to us in the Christmas story.

D. God's gift of love is what the world needs most. What greater gift could have been given to the people who came to Bethlehem? The greatest gift any of us can receive during this holy season is the overwhelming love of God.

## III. Love Changes Lives

A. Look what the acceptance of God's love did in the lives of those who are mentioned in the Christmas story. Zechariah and Elizabeth's life was never the same again. Mary and Joseph had a very special Child and memories they treasured. The shepherds were still shepherds but had a new outlook on life. The wise men were wiser than ever.

B. The acceptance of God's love will change your life as well.
  1. Illustration: A gift is not ours until we open it and take ownership.
  2. Love, joy, peace, and confidence await your acceptance.

## Conclusion

The greatest lesson we can learn from Christmas is the difference God's love makes in the lives of those who participate in the experience.

## Close with a Carol

"Silent Night! Holy Night!"

# LESSONS FROM THE CHRISTMAS STORY—MESSAGE FIVE

## Luke 2:21-52

### Introduction

A. Christmas Day is over for this year. But the lessons we can learn from this holy season continue. The range of characters in the Christmas story goes from the rich and wise to the poor and lowly.

B. The key personalities in this story are Mary and Joseph.
   1. The manner in which God used a peasant girl and a humble carpenter to bring His Son, Jesus, into this world has much to say to us about how God chooses to deal with ordinary people.
   2. We must never forget that Mary and Joseph are pivotal to the drama of our redemption.
   3. This scripture passage is lengthy, but it is God's Word. Read Luke 2:21-52.

## I. Lesson One Is the Beauty and Joy That Are the Results of Total Commitment

A. We need to go back before today's scripture to learn how Joseph and Mary were able to become God's vessels that He could use.
   1. Mary's total commitment is stated in Luke 1:38. Blessed are those who learn to rejoice in God's will whether or not they understand it.
   2. Joseph's total commitment is stated in Matt. 1:24.
   3. Young people today still will be wise to allow the Lord to work out all of the details of their lives—particularly in the choice of their spouses.

B. The commitment of Mary and Joseph continued after the birth of Jesus.
   1. They kept the faith that had brought them together.
   2. In Luke 2:21-22 we read that they were careful to keep the provisions of their faith.
   3. They set before Jesus an example that showed that God's ways are vital to our lives.

C. It would be wonderful if this lesson could be a contagious part of our lives today.

## II. Lesson Two Is That God Continues to Guide Those Who Are Pursuing His Will
A. God led Mary and Joseph to Egypt (Matt. 2:13).
1. God knew what Herod would do and directed Joseph accordingly.
2. Joseph displayed the faith of Abraham in taking his family to a strange land.
B. God led them to Galilee (vv. 19-22).
C. Once the pattern of obedience is established, God continues to give leadership. We know that Prov. 3:5-6 means that we cannot ignorantly miss God's will. Wherever Joseph was, God could communicate with him because Joseph was listening.

## III. Lesson Three Is That Jesus Can Be Easily Lost
A. The trip to Jerusalem 12 years after Christmas illustrates this (Luke 2:41-50).
1. They were following the customary activities of the day.
2. On journeys of this kind the people always traveled in large groups.
3. In the Temple Jesus never left them. They left Him.
4. Verse 44 shows us that Jesus must not be taken for granted.
5. Jesus was found where they left Him.
B. We must be careful that we do not take Jesus for granted in our world. There are many things that can crowd Jesus out of our lives. Wake up! Where is Jesus in your life? If Jesus is missing, you will find Him where you left Him.

## Conclusion
I hope you have learned the practical truths of the beautiful story of Christmas. Learning these lessons will make the coming new year the best year of your life.

## Close with a Song
"Trust and Obey"

# Part VI

# Messages That Are Not Part of a Series

The outlines in this section are prepared to be preached as "stand alone" messages. This means that since there is no sequence involved, any one sermon can be used at any time during the Christmas season. They will help focus attention on the advent of the Christ child and the importance of keeping the season.

# Let's Keep Christmas

## Luke 2:1-20

**Introduction**
- A. We live in a day of changes. There have been great changes in the standard of living. There are even changes in conduct and behavior. There have been many changes in religious concepts.
- B. There is one thing that has not been changed and must not be changed. That is the message of Christmas.
  1. Although nonbelievers have tried to change the Christmas message, they cannot do that.
  2. It would be easier to change the colors of Christmas than it would be to change its message.

## I. Why Seek Something New?
- A. There is no need to search for a new and different story. Only one story rings true. Read the Christmas story from Luke 2:1-20.
- B. We feel the pressure of Christmas.
  1. We wrestle with the problems of buying presents. Why not give the most precious gift of all—love?
  2. There are many other things that cannot be purchased in a store that are treasured gifts—kindness, patience, and so on.

## II. Christmas Is Often Crowded Out
- A. Be on guard so that you do not permit the rush of Christmas to crowd out the real Christmas from your heart.
- B. Some people complain that Christmas is just for the children. This shows they never really understood what Christmas was about. The older we get, the more Christmas means to us.
- C. Some people say they just cannot feel the Christmas spirit. The solution to this complaint is to read the story over and over again.

### III. Thank God for Christmas

A. It would be great if Christmas lasted throughout the entire year. On Christmas the whole world is a better place to live. Miracles happen because of the love that fills the hearts of people.

B. It is a wonderful time of family togetherness and happiness.

1. Traditions such as decorating the tree can be very meaningful.
2. The fun of hidden presents, forbidden closets, and bulging overcoats enhances the anticipation.
3. The fragrance of the baking and cooking that take place makes the home smell better.
4. The melodious strains of the carols are restful and inspiring.

C. Christmas morning will arrive. Somehow you will be ready. Someway the spirit will get you whether you get "it" or not. You will remember the true meaning of Christmas.

### IV. The Promise of the Angels Is True Today

A. They brought the promise of peace on earth.

1. It is not a pronouncement upon the state of the world.
2. It is God's promise of what His plans are for the earth.
3. Bethlehem is the only way to real peace.

B. We long for the love among men of goodwill that the season brings. We enjoy the miracles that are performed in the hearts of people. Many discover that their family ties are strengthened.

C. The promise of the angels when fulfilled in our lives changes our world.

### Conclusion

We will not spend or observe Christmas but keep it in all of the loveliness of its tradition. May we keep it in our hearts so that we may be kept in its hope.

### Close with a Carol

"The First Noel"

# What Will You Give Jesus?

## Matthew 2:1-12

### Introduction

   A. All of us tend to get caught up in the shopping mania that takes place at Christmas. Some may have finished. Most of us still have some shopping to do.

   B. I enjoy all of Christmas—even the giving and receiving part. I am in no hurry to finish with Christmas.

      1. Christmas makes the world a better place in which to live.

      2. In World War I the opposing armies took a 24-hour period of peace on Christmas Eve.

      3. At Christmas people sing happy and exciting songs.

      4. Many people finally realize that there are needy people around us and reach out to help them.

   C. The question of what to give was solved in our first Christmas. Read Matt. 2:1-12.

### I. Let's Look at Gifts and Christmas

   A. I hope that you get all of your shopping done so that you can take some time to reflect upon the beauty of Christmas.

      1. Do not lose sight of the importance of gifts.

      2. Gifts are a vital part. That's how it all started. Read John 3:16 and Rom. 5:8.

   B. Just think of what God has given to you—forgiveness of sins, peace, love, self-respect.

      1. God's gift to me was the most valuable one I ever received.

      2. What God has given to me is still good and gets better each year.

### II. The Wise Men Gave Gifts to Jesus

   A. The story of the wise men is told in the Scriptures.

      1. There are many questions that arise concerning these men. Who were they? Where did they come from?

2. The significance of their gifts.
   a. Gold—the most appropriate gift for a king
   b. Frankincense—the gift for a priest
   c. Myrrh—a gift for one who would die
   B. There are some things about these men that we know for certain.
   1. Since anyone who follows the best light available is wise, they were truly wise men (vv. 2, 9, 10, 12).
   2. All who search for Jesus until they find Him are wise. They searched for two years. Anyone who offers his best to God is wise. They did (v. 11).

## III. Wise Men Still Act This Way
   A. Wise men still follow the best light they can find.
   1. These men did not know Jesus' story but recognized that something special was taking place.
   2. You know the story. Are you following the light that God has given to you?
   3. First John 1:7 is God's promise of a great experience that comes from following our Light.
   4. Walking in darkness can be dangerous.
   5. God has illuminated a Star so that you can walk in His light.
   B. Wise men still search until they find Jesus.
   1. There were many discouragements in the pathway of the first wise men as they traveled.
   2. If we were giving the first wise men advice, we would say, "Keep going. Your journey will be worth the effort."
   C. Wise men give Jesus the best they have. Our best is good enough for Him.
   1. All Jesus ever asked for is what people have.
   2. Illustration: Tell about the lad's lunch, Peter's boat, and so on.
   3. What is the best you have?

## Conclusion
   Is Jesus on your gift list? Be sure that you include Him so that you can make the most of Christmas. The best gift you can give Him is yourself.

## Close with a Carol
   "O Come, All Ye Faithful"

# LET US GO TO BETHLEHEM

## Luke 2:1-20

### Introduction
    A. Invitations are peculiar things.
        1. We accept some out of courtesy.
        2. We accept some in anticipation of a great experience.
        3. We pass up some and are happy we did.
        4. We later regret we missed out on some of the invitations we declined.
        5. The occasion of the invitation is what determines its value.
    B. The invitation to Bethlehem was very special. Read the scripture, Luke 2:1-20.

### I. Let's Take a Look at Those Who Accepted the First Invitation to Bethlehem
    A. Heavenly beings were in attendance.
        1. The Bethlehem experience caught the attention of the angels of God.
        2. While angels have no problem, even they rejoiced over the incident at Bethlehem.
        3. The hillside was covered and the stable crowded with heavenly beings.
    B. Plain people came to Bethlehem.
        1. The invitation covered people from all walks of life.
        2. Lowly shepherds from the hill country accepted the invitation and went to Bethlehem.
        3. These plain people were given a wonderful privilege, and they took advantage of this.
        4. They had an exciting experience (v. 20).
        5. Most of us are in the shepherds' class of the people invited to meet Christ.
    C. People of royal birth came to Bethlehem.
        1. These represent those who come from the elite areas of life.

    2. It is important to understand that no one is left out of the invitation to experience Christ.

  D. Illustration: Tell about how people from every walk of life have come to know Jesus Christ.

## II. Let's Look at the Results That Come from Accepting the Invitation to Bethlehem

  A. Those who were involved in the first Christmas rejoiced.
    1. The angel chorus sang (vv. 13-14).
    2. The shepherds were blessed in their hearts (v. 20).
    3. The wise men rejoiced all the way to Bethlehem (Matt. 2:10).

  B. Today, those who go to Bethlehem in their hearts have great experiences.
    1. Just as the angels saw Jesus as heaven come to earth, so do we when we go to Bethlehem.
    2. Just as the shepherds saw Him as the Savior of humankind, so do we.
    3. Just as the kings saw Him as Ruler of the universe, so do we.

## Conclusion

  A. The shepherds and kings accepted their invitations and had wonderful experiences.
  B. Let us accept our invitation to Christmas so that we, too, may have great experiences.

## Close with a Carol

"O Come, All Ye Faithful"

# The Greatness of Christmas

## Luke 2:1-20

### Introduction

The greatness of Christmas is lost to many people. There are so many little things attached to the Christmas experience that can squeeze out the greatest opportunities. By taking a fresh look at the Christmas story, we can learn four things that will help us keep our lives open to the flow of God's message.

### I. It Was the World's Greatest Event (vv. 1-7)

A. Many wonderful things have happened in the history of our world.

   1. When the children of Israel left Egypt and crossed the Red Sea, it was a great experience.

   2. The discovery of America was a great experience. A man walking on the moon was a great experience. There have been some great medical breakthroughs.

B. These verses (1-7) describe the greatest event of all.

   1. Jesus was born in an inn to signify that He had only come to stay in this world for a short time.

   2. In the same way that an inn receives all guests, Jesus hangs out a banner of love to signify His welcome to all who come.

   3. Jesus was born in a stable where cattle were fed to show He would be the Bread of Life.

   4. The clothes in which Jesus was wrapped signify that the King of the universe became poor so that we might become rich. Could any other event in world history ever compare to this?

### II. It Was the World's Greatest Announcement (vv. 8-14)

A. Illustration: When Prince Charles of England was born, a great announcement was made. Since it was the announcement of the birth of the next king of England, everyone rejoiced. On November 14, 1948, at 10 P.M., thousands of people were waiting outside when the announcement was made that a king had been born. The bells in St. Paul's Cathedral and Westminster Abbey rang incessantly. The following day, trading on the Stock Exchange paused so that they could sing "God Save the King." To make sure everyone knew, 21- and 41-gun salutes were given to hail the birth of the new king. It was truly a great announcement.

B. The announcement of the birth of the King of the universe was greater than that one. Since this birth affected the entire universe, God placed a special star in the sky. Since He would bring great joy, a marvelous choir of angels sang the announcement.

## III. It Was the World's Greatest Message (vv. 10-14)

A. No other message could ever affect the world as this one.
   1. The announcement of a solution to humankind's greatest problem, the sin problem, was made (v. 11).
   2. The announcement that there can be peace in our lives while living on this earth was made (v. 14).

B. In spite of its greatness, God sent a personal message to everyone who reads it (v. 11). This is a message of forgiveness for all of our sins. It is a message that brings freedom from the bondage of sins.

## IV. This Message Evoked the Greatest Response (vv. 15-17)

A. This great message demands a response.

B. The shepherds reacted to the first message in a positive way. They became acquainted with Christ by following the guidance of the message. They shared the message with others after they had received it (v. 17).

C. Each one of us can react in the same way by having a personal encounter and then by sharing that with others.

## Conclusion

Christmas is the greatest day in the history of the world. Do not let the small things of life rob you of the maximum enjoyment of this experience. Let us celebrate the coming of Christ.

## Close with a Carol

"Joy to the World"